THE BOAT
THAT BROUGHT SADNESS
INTO THE WORLD

poems by

Eva Skrande

Finishing Line Press
Georgetown, Kentucky

THE BOAT
THAT BROUGHT SADNESS
INTO THE WORLD

Copyright © 2024 by Eva Skrande
ISBN 979-8-88838-614-9 First Edition
All rights reserved under International and Pan-American Copyright Conventions. No part of this book may be reproduced in any manner whatsoever without written permission from the publisher, except in the case of brief quotations embodied in critical articles and reviews.

Publisher: Leah Huete de Maines
Editor: Christen Kincaid
Cover Art: Elizabeth Josephson
Author Photo: Eva Skrande
Cover Design: Elizabeth Maines McCleavy

Order online: www.finishinglinepress.com
also available on amazon.com

Author inquiries and mail orders:
Finishing Line Press
PO Box 1626
Georgetown, Kentucky 40324
USA

Contents

THE BOAT THAT BROUGHT SADNESS INTO THE WORLD 1

SECTION 1

WHY THIS.. 5

LILIES 6

PROPHECY 7

THE LILACS 8

STATUES 9

SCARECROW ROAD 10

THE CHURCHES 11

ORACLE 12

NOTE 13

SECTION 2

NIGHT... 17

GHAZAL 18

DESCENDANT 19

LIES 20

TULIP 21

MARROW 22

CROWS... 23

IN THE LIGHT OF DAY 24

THE GARDEN 25

OPPOSITES 26

WEATHERVANE IN THE DIRECTION OF WHY 27

BREAD.. 29

THE RIVER 30

IN RIVERS	31
THE HORSE	32
ORCHID	33
THE PEONIES	34
SECTION 3	37
BREEZE	39
THE HOUSE	40
THROW YOURSELF LIKE WATER	41
SPIRIT, GIVE ME	43
THE BOAT	45
THIS ASTONISHING WORLD	46
EYE LEVEL	47
THE SEA	48
ENEMIES	49
WHEN THE NIGHT COMES IN	50
THE WALLS	51
HAPPY ARE THOSE	52
CABALETTA	53
LACE	54
AERIALIST	55
THE HYDRANGEA	56
DESTINY	57
ALL FOREVERS	58
HONEY	59
SUNDAY	60
THE HUMMINGBIRDS	61
BIRDS	62
THE HOUSES	64

For Ben and Paloma

THE BOAT THAT BROUGHT SADNESS INTO THE WORLD

The boat that brought sadness into the world
Arrived at night, the ocean dark
With the barely new moon, and one lone gull

Dipping its beak in and out of the water.
At the long end of the wharf, the fishermen
Waited among empty nets, and the smell of old fish.

The bells rang empty in the church tower,
The lighthouse bowed its head.
At that moment, of the half-asleep moon,

Fathers and mothers began to die.
Lovers watched as the few stars turned from the face
Of eternity.

The boat that brought sadness into the world
Had passed the boat of happiness,
Lingering by the horizon.

It was a simple boat, one of the gray boats.
Upon arriving, its sail turned
Into Memory, long and white.

SECTION 1

WHY THIS

I am neither salt nor earth, but I did give birth to a church which I traded
for all the hydrangea in worlds of bone

the way I traded an amethyst ring
once for a balloon, the ring I hid between my legs before officials checked

my hands for jewelry when
we were leaving an occupied country.

My poor arms had already practiced being an altar
the rest of me, jasmine. My birds are thick-skinned

especially around lions. So mother warned me:
bows and arrows are only for those who cannot carve boats out of wind.

So she said: make my memories honest ones. Then she turned into fire,
    leaving me
to grieve ants. What wolves me is hunger, the lack

of air surrounding the teeth of my boats.

LILIES

When I try too hard, my legs wilt:
like rose petals unaccustomed to sin. Then I become granules of blue bone.
At the very least, I am useful:
all cells of me unite into a church for the homeless corn.

I start where I always start: in the nave of the throat
where the hymns of fish decree that stars shall ride on their backs forever and
    ever.

My flowers, like mothers, warned me to walk straight to practice
going towards the sun with books on my head.
But I wanted to forgive roses their thorns,
to bend like water telling secrets.

I grew up in the presence of many moons,
some oracular some red with the energy of horses. I slept
in homes other than my own
to observe the sabbaths. Despite all the bad luck—the rain, the wind, my arched
    back—

I grew up with a mouth full of lilies.
They were not afraid of my teeth.

PROPHECY

All the quaint towns of my throat are open and ready for the white weather
    of lilies.
Love, you see, can travel on wings. For this reason, the night exhales
    butterflies.

What more can I be but forest, oracular:

the lion's feet are too narrow for my valleys,
but fit into my rivers:

if you want
to write songs with the blue ink of bones, pronounce my manna correctly.

My giving birth to stars is hereditary. I will kiss the ground they fall on.

Our hearts will have two lives: one during the dawn of daylilies.
One with the same last name as earth.

THE LILACS

When it is Friday night, and we are at home
the talk is about the lilacs how calm they are how patient
how they fall out of the pockets of scarecrows in order
to bring good luck to the mothers and fathers of corn.

Sometimes there are so many crows, the corn forgets its birthday
forgets the wedding of seed and soil
all anniversaries.

I, like corn, have crows that want my kernels of bone
the crows of sweeping and cooking the crows of bills and debt
the days when my mother didn't come home until late

from solving the equations of corn and crows:
(It is possible for the hands to turn blue waiting for mother.)
days when the moon of a heart speaks solely
above ravened roads.

The corn and I want to be saved from all our crows. This is why
my scarecrows wear a necklace of lilacs.
But, sometimes, even lilacs stutter.

STATUES

Along the road of memory, there are statues of fire and the closed hands of a
    child praying.

I see the burnt body of my mother, lying on the hospital bed,
like an island of white gauze.

Fire is good to memory as one thing it can't forget.

Then, there's a youth of prayer, for the Sabbath,
for the new month and, sometimes, for the full moon

lighting up the wheat and all its mothers who haven't burned.

What dress to wear to honor memory, what shoes, what purse?

When the trees fear fire and hum the prayers
for their upcoming fruits,
I cry.

SCARECROW ROAD

They grew as cornstalks

    heavy with dusk.

The orchestra of stars and corn, blue and aware

    of their dishonesty.

No bone

    in the cave of their mouth:

because of the trumpets of hay, a heart.

How many eyes are there in the word crow?

    In the word women?

In all the crossroads of fields, it is important to consider

    epistles of gravity and wing.

At night, the crows who can't see the scarecrow, but believe it is there, take their chances.

    We are all body for our believers,

we crow for light.

THE CHURCHES

All day, my hands sway back and forth like the fins of minnows
in the fishbowls of memory.

I wish it was future already: but my horses and moons disagree.

My mother's last letter said:
I am here to tell you what happens to lilies

when they no longer have throats: each petal breaks into a million lions.
This was the earth's testament:

that churches would open in the fields of daisies, churches where children
    find sanctuary. Picture this:

and all mothers shall be safe
from the teeth of lions, teeth which keep falling out

but reappear where crows tell their stories to the river. And the boats,
especially the red ones, claimed to be the dresses of fortune.

ORACLE

When the corn refuses   its own echo,
           and the rivers

want to be honest about depressed mothers,
the bones refuse to speak in any language.
Once I opened my mouth
            and a storm of crows rushed in.

I wanted to save a piece of my mother's hair as proof
            she once lived,

but her scorched hair   fell apart in my hands.
Even the corn
            knows this.

My mother believed in the sermons of boats. One time,
she extended her arms to hug the river, but

            she only heard the foghorns behind her.

The crows love fire, love the alphabet in sad hearts.
The lilacs have learned to avoid fire

            especially when the river calls in its crows,

when the night's cup fills with ash.

NOTE

Am I being honest
                when I tell you
                my bones are blue:
                this is why I float in water

and my arms are always asking questions of the fish.

It is important
        to count the heart's fish early, not just when the first star is heard in
   the night

or when the first candle is lit among the teeth of refugees.

        Candles argue that every dance
in the throats of birds is a lie. It's possible

for all three of our hands to be angry
        to whisper like waves abandoned on the shore overnight.
        I would
   say

the mouth is a birdhouse for the architecture of lost wolves,
for seabirds gone wing.

SECTION 2

NIGHT

Come here, night, wrap your arms
around my softly elated body. Tonight,
I am an old piano suddenly awake

toward the serene feet of stars.

Sweet night, you water my forehead's asters.
I drink the constellations

that light all the lily-filled fields of Jerusalems within me.
I am grateful heavens.

You are an accordion that inhales
and exhales the dreams of lost tulips.
The moon rests its kisses on the tips of your blue wheat.

Dear night, let just-born birds learn to fly from my eyelids.

For my sake, please,
let only the suffering die this beautiful night.

GHAZAL

First the birds, knowing, flap their wings.
Then playful orchids are called home as if for dinner.

Stars go out like someone closing a book
and turning off the light before going to sleep.

The wind walks lost through the world,
hungry for bread.

O crying trees of the park inside me. O mist
turning the blaze of lampposts into white questions.

Look, already before the dawn, birds
tap at the window of the next world.

The sounds of a guitar in the distance. Shall we dance—
what light remains of you, and myself?

DESCENDANT

The night bellows out of me like a descendant.
The moon telling its remembrances
above the dark field of my throat.

In the birdhouse behind my eyelid, your voice
sings of the shore of the eternal.
There are palm fronds left dancing between my fingers.

LIES

        I was a baby born in the arms of a tree.
                I had no grandmother, not even
a father or mother.
The few caps I wore, I threw
      into a headless river.

            I was a boat born
                    without food or wine.
    I swam amongst the flotsam of stars.
                 I had only four fingers

to hold the moon.

      I was a window, a church
an old pair of shoes, an owl in the martyrdom
of night.

I became a flower.
      I had one ear to listen for enemies.

    I became a song. I became a heart, lucky and green.

                 I became a liar.
      I rewrote my past.
On the last page of my life
      I lulled the wind to sleep
                in my arms.

TULIP

Another day of carrying burdens on my back—
tired stars, old trees, and numerous pasts.
There are cries on my back, too, like the tears of hundreds

of exiles passing by their homeland on distant boats.

All I know of days is the clock of my steps. All I know
of evenings is the darkness under my feet. I walk along

cities whose winds refuse to be calm.
Every now and then, I stop to adjust my burdens

like refugees who carry everything they can in blankets
tied together on their backs. I want

a house, new or old, in the homeland of my childhood. I want
dear seas to open inside me, to plant apple trees and tulips,
and plenty of milk to give to orphaned children.

Once I carried only the whispers of rivers on my back.
Now, I trip over the murmurs of stones in the road.

O large and eternal tulip,

how long till my burdens fall off me—
how many lost stars must bend me over
before my shoulders dance, again, like free birds?

MARROW

Once again crabgrass grows between the cracks in the long sidewalk of
    someone's life.
The curb bends its back like a person overwhelmed
by the fear of poverty's sad garments.

Because it's not easy this world.
Despite children, despite boats,
despite everything that has learned to walk without crutches.

In the cold, old men wear their coat collars high around their heads.
Still the snow lands on eyelashes like forbidden sins.

The marrow of evening turns the river dark.
Meanwhile, I am a pale boat on the water, roofless, a few refugees asleep
on the pillows of night.
The scared children's wide-open eyes lighting the world.

CROWS

I carry days, months, and years all at once,
all this heaviness as a wanderer
between bitterroot and bread. When it rains,
I cannot turn the wet pages of life.
When the finches lining my roads sing,
the song of corn wakes inside me. Then
I become all scarecrow—
I hold my straw like a sweet yoke,
my shoes too small for any long journey.
These are days whose bellies fill with corn
and the sighs of wind. I am happiest
when I am the savior in the temple of corn,
despite the gray topography of days
and the burden of crows. O torches of being,
I shall set my days by the banks of willing.
Already, though, I'm tired, my straw bones
refusing their names. Still, I brush my hair
for the caravan of tomorrows,
my future written on the wings of crows.

IN THE LIGHT OF DAY

In the light of day, I die.
The wheat's green eyes close
for their heavenly rest.
Already, I wear a towel of clouds
around my hips, and a blouse
made of the dropped feathers of birds.
The cups of the town's beggars fill, today,
with jasmine and gold. When the far-off bell rings,
hundreds of tulips, ready
for the new world, will leave my chest.
The body of the river will rise, almost bowing.
Tree limbs will begin filling with the buds of sleep.
The manna falling will be enough
to feed forever all who are hungry.

THE GARDEN

                  I knelt on the ground to listen to the talk of the flowers—
their childhoods,   the dances,   whatever keeps them from sadness.
Above all,
        they love the sway of sun.

    I tried to make sure they would always have rain, mulch, and nectar
                                          to kiss with.
I cared for them
        as I would an elegant dress.
They forgave my trespasses,
        my belief in wind   instead of sin.

        Next to the nigella and dahlias,
                already losing their petals,
I wondered how long the petals
        inside me
                would last.
I wanted to be like flowers,
        letting go of their petals
                almost gracefully,
like one who is certain she will be alive the next day
        slowly takes off an evening gown
    then goes to sleep.

                        Even the flowers seem to trust
    that, despite being cut or caught in storms, their families
of lilies, begonias, nasturtiums

will always come after them.
I, too, want to grow forever,
        turning into this or that root, this or that flower

                but not yet, holy power, not yet.

OPPOSITES

There's the beauty, of course, of one and negative one,
        moon and negative moon, a mountain

and the good feet of the righteous valley
        below it. Even the dark cave

of the mouth has its own flicker of rose—
        even the darkness has its own speck

of candle. There's the round prayer of Ferris
        wheels versus the straight breath of ladders

the soft prayer of a child kneeling next to her bed
        against the loud cry of the repentant thief

which is beautiful enough to make the unbelieving
        coat on the clothes rack fall to its knees,

because that flock of birds flying out of sight in the sky
        will always be visible to someone, somewhere.

WEATHERVANE IN THE DIRECTION OF WHY

I am made of countries
               and bone.
        Made of the wishes
of juniper and pine
      of the promises told to the exiled
              by brine and embittered snow.
I am all pilgrim,
    a weathervane in the direction of why.
      Each star, each small cell
         of night
    beckons me forward,
beckons forth
      my homeland. All atoms combine
            to make me
weaver and book.
      I am a book of rinds.
I have two hearts
         ready
    to swim upon notice,
one to help me float if necessary,
      one to accompany me
to a gathering
    of boats.
          An island made of dolls in old dresses.
Ask me to sing, and I'll fly.
        I am made up of wanderers
         who read the moons carefully
looking for signs
    of manna and rain.
      I am made up of empty casinos,
of the night as a roulette wheel.
      I am a growing blanket
    of nostalgia,
I cry for the roofs
    of my past,
        for unsworn sabbaticals.
I wear three languages:
    of copper, coal, and cobalt.

                I am made up of oceans,

all five of them.
        I am made up of lampposts
that rise from oceans,
                eager to place bets
    on what is infinite and dark.

BREAD

Each day, I eat my portion of bread
spread with doubt and unknowing.
Always praying for the sake of my orchards.

My small house, by the beach, loves the piano of waves
despite their dutiful dirge.
The old windows carry their cargo of rain and snow

but fear the patter of memories,

and my table knows the weight
of apples and gloom. When I eat,

the old chalices join me. They are eager
to bless the wine made of burdens and sad stars.

If lost driftwood, the history of all my seas,
knocks at the door, I invite it in.
Then, I am all flotsam.

I open my door to all prophets,
let all who are lonely and fleeing
their own sad centuries

come and eat.
We wash our hands before we bless the bread
and sing in praise of the sea grape trees

for how well they carry their age, for how well,
despite growing along the shore,

they withstand the jetsam of life.

THE RIVER

When the river decides to gather
in the small of my back
bringing all her fish,
I dream of you, old love,
dipping your toes into the river,
then slowly your face.
Your hands, like small fish,
can do anything they want there—
build a water castle for the fish
cup the water, green from the trees
along the bank,
offering it to the smiles of fate.
And you learn to speak the language
of fish, you know how
to open your heart there
taking in the dreams of water.
You know how to swim there
despite the shallowness of my back
and the plentiful fish,
despite the shortness of this life
and that we are fish only once.

IN RIVERS
          after Sherwin Bitsui

When we river, our long hair spreads blue
within the banks of manna. The breezes

along our riverback
open their mouths at the feet of reeds
that don't believe in sin. And the moon,

that lovely fruit, whispers songs into the faces
of swimmers turning toward silver. Rivering,

we don't regret the loud fish of the past, we enjoy
the white caps of memory,

let the chest carry its beautiful burden of bluegills

to our banks gracefully.
Our marshes are grateful
to be blessed with yellow breaths.

Boats held up by our fingers carry corn to those with old hearts.

When we river,
the holy night crests at our elbows.

THE HORSE

Every day, I ride the wild horse of fear.
No saddle is good enough, no stirrups or reins.

There is no oasis among the hills of unknowing
I can take it to.
It rears up and shakes its head

certain it knows the future in the calvary of life.

When the rains come without end,
it keeps trying to buck me off.

No flowers can soften its heart. It refuses

the stable I have built out of wood and doubt
for it to sleep.

I want to ride the stubborn horse into a giant flower,
to the center,
petal after gentle petal surrounding me,

nothing leading me
toward this or that fail, to this or that fall.

ORCHID

What have you become, my Cuba, my orchid of a homeland,
besides the stray hairs of my dreams.
I am missing three fingers for this journey

of exiled peonies and bees.

I wish I could once again see
your benches where the weary come to sit

and watch their burdens bloom into butterflies.

I miss the parks under your bridges, the brides walking down
the aisle under canopies of palm trees.

O water of infinite blue

splashing on the shoulders of your cities.

I want to see the cathedral in the plaza
where men go to wash their feet

and women baptize their hopes. If only I could

find my old house in the streets of your capital
to feel sparrows in the eaves of my heart.

Exiles cry, sweet land, for the white rapture of doves

within your gardens. Even those who are tired are happy
along orchid-filled streets, and pigeons take turns kissing
the stones of your old roads.

What boats lead back to the fruits of your hands—O dear country,

on what knees did you bid us farewell?

THE PEONIES

When I was a child, butterflies landed
                        on my shoulders and fingers.
There were hens and roosters
                           to watch in my neighbor's yard
               and lightning bugs,   like low stars
                                 pulled out by a magician
from the black hat of night.

               I walked with a limp
                       to mimic my grandmother.

I had no idea the large,   open   mouth of exile
                               would swallow me whole
       or that refugees hid wedding rings
                     in the heels of their shoes.
I didn't know the sadness
              of leaving her country,   the kind that weighs on you
    like an earth,
      would break
                my mother. I worried
a new language would fail my tongue.

                  I spent long hours on the swings of exile
      unaware that the country
             of my body   was filled with silent violins.

              I was scared
of dark petals falling off flowers,   snakes,
           and deep oceans of hurt.   When my grandmother died,

        I learned to fear death.

Now,   on the porch of old age,
                     I watch the fully opened peonies in the garden

and wonder how long they will last
                        in the orchestra of life.
                        O sweet chants of cellos

in the distance, let it be a long time
                        before they are exiled
                                      from the pink orb of their bodies.

SECTION 3

BREEZE

In the space between the horizon and the blink of an eye
light is born. A thousand red lilies glow
in the river of morning.
The mouths of shadows begin opening as if to sing.

In the afternoon, the swings of memory awaken
in the parks of old age.
Roads toward this or that suffering are restless.
Still the world seeks its purpose gazing at your back.

At dusk, purple light lands on your body.
Rooftops rest from looking upward.
Houses close inward, gather their wings.
O breeze, rolling through the bushes of life.

Come evening, leaves fall gently off trees.
Stars are covered, now, by clouds.
The night assumes its gesture of habit. It is too cold
for birds to loosen themselves from the sins of your hair.

THE HOUSE

I want to find my childhood home
among the hydrangea,   the daylilies   and peonies.   There
where the bowl on the dining room table is always filled
with pomegranates, pears, and luck

where the roof sings its song
for those who have nothing, and all who look in its windows
                        are promised
                        to never be exiled again.

There are boats in the nearby river
with good hearts,   birds in the trees
who believe in prayer and dawns.
                        The pear trees ripen away from debt.

I want to play, again, on the swing next door
                        and look over the backyard wall
                        to see the neighbors' roosters and hens,
anything free of doubt and worry.

                        O sweet house,
there are no horses left who know how to get to you.   And I,
I walk as a tourist in my own dreams,
                    where the stars are barely lit
                    and palm trees keep calling my name.
I miss my house, now,
          in old age
          when there are more birds in back of me than in front.

THROW YOURSELF LIKE WATER
after Miguel de Unamuno

Throw yourself   like water   to the dry fields

where the wheat dreams
         of love.

Or into June and July like soft rain. Throw yourself

               like a gazelle of light
               into the room of a child afraid
               of the dark.

Forget the lone house   at the end of the road

     or worrying about which broom you will use
     to sweep the cobwebs in the corner

of memory's porch.

Throw yourself   like a dove

into the soft light just after dawn. Throw yourself

like a moon onto the dark path of refugees,
             like a heart into the calling body

               of the three-day-old daffodil.
               Throw yourself like soil
               to grow what has yet to be,

like trust into the field of everything
             you were denied—the boats,
             dinner among the daylilies,

the bright-blue world of the round hydrangea.

Throw yourself like fire into the river of extinguished stars,　like hope
　　　　　　　　　　into a valley filled with
　　　　　　　　　　　　　　　thunder and debt.
　　　　　　　　　　　　　　Throw yourself

　　　　like morning　　　　into the cells of those unfairly jailed

like love into the emptiness of newly-orphaned roses.

SPIRIT, GIVE ME
after Juan Ramón Jiménez

Spirit, give me the ability to become a boat where there is no song.
                                        Give me the opportunity
to believe in a world whose pages turn slowly
when there is debt.
                Teach me
how to carry my suitcase of memories
                        on my back

when I am afraid of dusk.   Enable me to walk

without sadness
from one bridge to another in the gardens of melancholy.

                                        Show me what to do
if others hurt me. Allow me to open windows
                when the chambers of the heart
are dark with smoke.

                        If I can never stop wandering,
                let it be on blue horses.

Allow me to believe for the second time
                                in the innocence of daylilies.

Forgive me for the lions of my mountains,   for turning away
from the footprints of blind candles.

                                Teach me to love rivers even if
sometimes I must cross them
to get to my finches.
                Help me make an altar of stars
                        to bow in front of the evening
even if
I can't afford a dress and new shoes.   Forgive me
                                        my leaning house.
Escort me to the hives
                where bees make their honey

that I may see their churches
and pray in the language of tulips.   Help me to understand

that, despite the body I've been given,

                                                         I am only the dream

of roses.

THE BOAT

Each time another friend dies,   death inhabits me more and more,
first by turning off lamps in the dark corners
                of the body, or as a tree
dropping its last fruit
                        before winter.
It's the time of day after the table is set,
            and people stroll
                            by the window.
When life lacks an anchor to keep us in one place,
                when refugees
     are tired of walking,
        and even what's left   of the day's   bread weighs
     as much as a suitcase of fear.
                   Or it's early, when day is
       unmoored,   and refugees can no longer hide
                  in the boat of night.
Then I think of my own heart,   itself a boat,
                                          bobbing in the distance,
                    exiled on a starless night,
                                the seagulls of worry circling
   the docks.
It's the time when the sailors are more restless than usual.
            I know then
                    that death is on board,

               its coat hanging from a nail on deck,

a small breath enough
                  to make it stir.

THIS ASTONISHING WORLD
after Ángel González

This astonishing world   where we turn   to horses for their blue
    answers,
        where love cracks   as easily as glass,
            and trees whisper aubades
                  to the boats that leave for work each morning,
where bag ladies sit in the corners of rain, and the homeless
    look forward to loaves of fire
at night   when winter soaks their dreams,
where spiders threaten those in tattered shoes,
        and fever forms on the foreheads
of the wheat and its children.
                Look,
  the elderly sit on balconies and knit
            their memories into scarves,
    the daffodils mourn their mothers and fathers,
                    and old birds sing
to ward off death.
              O world astonishing
because we can rest our tired breaths   on hammocks between two pines,
    because sometimes
           the weathervanes move
           in the opposite direction
    of sadness,
               because even in refugee camps
              the children hide behind tents
              in a game of hide-and-seek,
because we can imagine blue horses
            and set an extra place at dinner
          for destiny,
            so we can ask her to let us always breathe easily
          and, if we can't,
    to make sure
we don't die alone.

EYE LEVEL

I am always in a race
        against wind and death
trying
    to hurdle past them
  as if birds with no wings
were possible,
      as if the stars could listen
            to calls for help. To outrun death,
my mother told me
        turn up the music of the gladioli
in the giant vase by the window
      because death hates music,
hates anything that reminds its birds
    of their grace.
        Along the roads and mountains
of this race,
    I have tripped often
over stones, tree roots
        and the sins of roses.
I've forgiven the bitterroot
      its heart of tumbleweed
and old salt.
      For years,
I've ignored the finish line.
          The kind garden of life
has given me many flowers.
      I've been saved by the empathy of euphorbia
and honeysuckle,   given breath after breath
of days instead of dust.
        Now, the finish line
rises more and more
      toward eye level. I live in fear
 of not breathing easily.
    It's hard, now, not to notice
the fields of dying wheat.
        I am one of the last stalks alive
in a field full
    of final breaths.

THE SEA

The place where I end
                and the great boatman begins
              is on shore
where an apple appears in the hands of a beggar,   where the pomegranate turns

toward sainthood,   and unwieldy boats bow
    at the grave of their mothers—

              perhaps it's the spot
        on a fevered forehead
                where birds leave their kisses
        or where frowns convert to

white roses on the faces of exiled children
        who have lost everything
          that sang to them, who wonder what happened
      who miss the swings and slides of their parks;

it's not far from the house
        that sinks with an unknown weight,
      or where smoke rises
     like the waltz of a beautiful dress in the wind. I, too,

began in the hands of my homeland
and travelled north, south, east, and west
              of Jerusalem's dreams—

    O let me dance in the choreography of sails,
let me swim, dress and all, in the sea
       where I can float sinless
             around the knees of boats
      where I can drift
         beyond the hem
            of my being.

ENEMIES

Of all my enemies,
the one that bothers me the most
                        is the rose that refuses
                        to break bread with me,

 or the old daisy
            that would rather listen
            to the night's
            songs,
                              even the fox who doesn't believe
in the trilogy of fish.
Then there's the clock
which rebuffs the blessings of my trees,
                    the garden that won't grow

any dawns,   or the lawn
                which whispers
that it's too late to dance with the moon.   There's also
                        the red sorrow
                        dressed up as one of my purses,

the fires burning all the windows of my cities,
              and the wind that threatens the eternity
            of my finches and their fountains.

Of course, there are the evenings
            that won't let me forget my own doubts   and the stars
                        which utter the names
                            of my enemies repeatedly
until I fill their dreams with milk and honey
                    until I sew enough clothes to keep them all warm

until, like the night,
                I can turn
                my other cheek.

WHEN THE NIGHT COMES IN
after Luis Rosales

When the night comes in, hundreds of refugees
climb quietly
        into boats.
                The moon
                and the coyote fall in love.
                When the night comes in,

the coat,
        in the corner of the room,
unloads its cold burdens.
When the night comes in, morning glories worry about debt.

        When the night comes in, those who are exiled
dream of finding their houses
in the land of their birth.
They cry, in their dreams,
                if they cannot find it.

When the night comes in, the nightingale softens
                the walk of madmen.

            When the night comes in,
swimmers are more careful   in the waves of doubt.
When the night comes in,
        stars hover
            over the homes of the lonely,
the cartographer falls asleep
on the mountainous land of sadness,
                the bullfighter hides his dark thoughts
                    in a red handkerchief. When the night comes in,
refugees
quickly unwind the rope from the dock.
        Suddenly
             the wolf's howl is a type of prayer.

THE WALLS

Four walls surround me,
                            four invisible walls

that keep me in bounds,
though I wish to go beyond them.   Yes,

                        within the walls,
                        palm fronds laugh with the wind

and pomegranates utter their red hopes,
but there is always debt, hunger, and cold.

Outside, is everything I want—

                        a simple pair of shoes, more trees, children,

and a house with flowers that never die.

I wish
these walls were collapsible,

I wish they had windows to let sun in
and doors to step through
to see trees form a canopy over the roofs of cottages,

houses full of finches,
where there is nothing to envy
because every morning there are boats full of song,
                                  songs that everyone can sing,

and fruits from which dancing seeds exit
so that no one is ever hungry
and there is always enough.

Fruit from which more fruit delicately grows.

HAPPY ARE THOSE

Happy are those in whose hands
                      the crepe myrtle and other June trees
open. Happy are those whose boats flower
with morning.
                Happy are those
who don't have to pretend
         there are windows in their tent homes.
Happy are those who are not alone
     among the valleys of death,
          in whose dreams a partner
they are unaware of awakens.
Happy is the bread in the oven,
     the pie cooling
on the kitchen counter,
          happy is everything that will become food
for those with nowhere to dock
their dreams.
       Happy are those who see yellow and pink mountains
and have blue horses
    to carry away the unwanted bricks
of memory.
      Happy are those whose pockets
are empty of bitterness,
who don't have to choose
     between darkness and light
       who have only a few loaves of bread
and accept their small portion.
Happy are those
           who don't cry for what could have been
in the old lands of their birth.
Happy are those
      who are not owners of earth,
        who go to bed certain they will wake up
who believe death has gone fishing
    in another continent of night.

CABALETTA

        A melody gallops
between trees,
filling the night with horses.

                Below the moon,
                bearers of sadness
                        want to dance

as if they, too, were horses galloping on

        despite the threat of cancer

or the memory of fire,

        led on by the dream of a wide field
        full of green grass,
        no rocks to hurt their feet,
        running toward each other,
        flowers in their mouths,

and the gallops, o the gallops

        creating a song

all the tall grass can dance to,
                that makes it possible to forget

the stroke of midnight

and tomorrow's work,

        to forget the heaviness
        on their backs,
        forget the burdens
                riding on their saddles.

LACE

To separate the soul
from the body,
          is an undressing: first

    skirt, then blouse
          and slip,
then
    the final lace
    of arms, etcetera, before

the soul comes into view.

It takes a certain willingness
to be like the rose

    in the garden, shedding its petals
    to be vulnerable, to forego
    the dishes and mopping,

to make room in a bed
where you are

and are not alone
    because the last petal of the last rose
        has come in through the window

to lie alongside you,
to teach you to discard your own
lace of petals

for the moment the horse appears,
to see the horse grazing,
    in love with pasture, grass,

    and the naked wind.

AERIALIST

There are times when
my roses are always listening
                      to the dirges in their garden
                      of sadness, when I have
a suitcase filled
with the trousers of sorrow. Then it constantly
rains, and my cup overflows
        with debt.
When I can no longer walk,
        I sit in a chair with only three legs.
At other times,
my house is full of finches,
        there is bread on the table,
            and the fork and knife want to marry.
                I have a broom
                to sweep away the cobwebs
                of fear. I don't need
light for the roads have no stones.
Then, my glasses of water
                      turn into great rivers,
and I'm ready
                to break joyously into flight,
                    to forget, for a moment, the anchors
holding me down.

THE HYDRANGEA

When the tables of life

                    are empty,
                    open wide the gates of gardens,
                    accept like refugees, the forks and knives of memory

bless the raging fathers and sick mothers,

remember that the drifting boats are guarded
                              by the compass-hearts of birds.

If there were fires in the pages of childhood,

                        set the table anyway, put a vase in the center
filled with the hard-won lessons of the hydrangea,

put heels on to greet the manna,
                        substitute the manes of stars for the uncut yards
                        sowed by the mistakes of history and bad
    teachers,
                        sing at the table for the lover who died,
      let in

the Friday-night brides knocking at the door.
Let the emptiness leave you. Sing, again,

              for the now open vessels of the heart, be grateful
              for the boats you wanted and were denied, light the candles
   as a
lighthouse

for the boat making its way to your table,

filled with honey and freed jasmine.

DESTINY

There are days when memory is a bull

I ride gracefully
         and days when I fall off and there is no bullfighter

to keep me
from remembering which tulips have died.
                                    There are days
cursed by fire and those filled with the blessings
of pomegranates and mangos.
                There are afternoons when I am all corn

                and afternoons when the crows come. Despite it all,

I am lucky
when there are no lions, and the bones can rest
from making sure bread is on the table. If the manna works, so be it.

If it doesn't, and the trees bear fruit, that will be enough.
                                Those who love me

must love my peaches and my pears. I will protect my finches
from those who hurt me.

Once hope was easy to read on the veins of leaves. Now
                      it's a wayward wind.

There are days I have worked empty fields,

roamed aimlessly
         within myself.
              I have been sister and brother to thorns.

If I could be something else,
                I'd be destiny
in an evening gown and heels
so I could decide my own future—not rain or debt
but days with a sunrise
                made solely of rubies and bouquets of red roses.

ALL FOREVERS

Inside the body, hummingbirds are possible.

Inside the body, I am all tree.

      I am open windows, I am light.
It is always a day of rest for my hummingbirds.

How lovely in the body
to be a hammock hoping for the little wind
of horses and groomsmen, to ask how many gallops

it takes to marry a silversmith.

In the body, I am all song:
like the sound of crows leaving me my summers.
            I am buttons for the torn coats of beggars.
            I am sailboat and harmony. Inside the body,

I am a good daughter to cathedrals I am happy to drown in.

I am roses, dresses, and feathers.
I am numbers and love the math of tricycles.

      I gather all my fractions.

I am all names, my hummingbirds.
I am all forevers.

When my Sunday dinners are ready, I am all bread.
         Let all who are hungry come and sit at my tables.

HONEY

Today, I cleanse my voice with rosemary
tomorrow thyme
and Sunday sage.

Life is honey.
The charging bulls have turned left
at the corner before mine

and the clouds have sent rain
to pay my debts.
I have been a duck, a street, and a tree.

Once I was even a beggar.
I have yet to be valley
or a pillar of salt

though I've been named migrant.
Of tulips, I am guilty
but the dew still collects in my hair

as if I were a rose or cathedral.
This is fun.
I want every joy

to hang from my wrists
as if in baskets,
I want to be the last name

of boats and peaches.
O thank you manna
for this respite from empty boulevards

for teaching me the names
of fertile countries.
I will kiss the dirt of my homelands,

pure fecund are my maps
my buckets of milk
and rivers.

SUNDAY
after Ángel González

Beautiful Sunday,
whose arms open to a thousand butterflies,
who returns memories of joyful carousels
to the minds of old trees
and cools the foreheads of fever, who gathers bag ladies
to sing alongside those dying alone
and loves the bored children in churches.
                Mother of sparrows,
who steers the boats,
barely awake, away from eddies,
and keeps the feet of refugees from tiring.
Even if it's just for one day
that the homes of the poor fill with bread and honey,
even if on Monday the backs of people bend over
while carrying suitcases of debt.
                O Jerusalem of days,
even if come Monday we forget
we promised you our right hand, even though we go back
to climbing hills, and move like donkeys
loaded with blankets, we look forward, again,
to your pomegranates and pears, vowing
not just our hands, but whole bodies filled
with a chorus of flowers
ready to harmonize with each of your dawns.

THE HUMMINGBIRDS

I'd rather be reading that *when they are born
hummingbirds*
               have no hair or feathers
than imagining
            the sinking heart
            of a child's paper boat.
I'd rather discover *that they can fly at three weeks of age*
            than think about the years it takes
            till we earn our feathers
so we can fly away
            from the owls of life.
            I'd rather learn *that newborn hummingbirds*
are approximately   *the same size as a penny*
            than consider
how few pennies   there are in a day
or that flowers open in the morning only
            to close at the first sight
of sorrow.
Let me read that the *hummingbird*
            is the only bird which can fly backwards
than believe
            the songs of birds can be colorless,
        than remember the refugees
        who can no longer carry birds
on their bent backs.   Like the hummingbird
            which *changes*
            from black to golden-green
on the back and crown   *with a gray-white belly,*
I will turn
            into other versions
            of myself.
        If I am fortunate
        my feathers, too, will get old.
All I ask is for my heart   to last as long as possible,
            that it be as strong
as the heart of the smallest bird
            which beats *1260* lucky times
        per minute.

BIRDS

thousands of birds live inside me

the marrow

of everything gentle

there are hundreds
                            for each year I have been fortunate to live

and many more waiting to be born
for the years

I still hope to be alive

                      sweet refugees that know only exile
in the days and nights of my body

in all my corners
and the magnolia trees of the heart

still they are lucky
                  they are safe from winter
debt and owls
they know nothing about wars
        or that flowers ultimately die

in the great vase of life
                  they live as in a cave full of nothing but jewels

they don't even know we are getting older
        they know nothing of the small distance

between beauty
and sad finches
        why should I tell them otherwise
I know

when they are singing
sometimes their wings flutter

then despite everything old

I am all wing

THE HOUSES

There are times my body walks by itself
    as if we were two stalks of wheat
            blowing in different winds.
 I straggle behind,
      like years do, with their memories
      of failed loves, of debts
         of dinners with no bread.
  My body
    strides ahead of me
      like a country seeking its name
        unconcerned   about the cartographer's struggles
        to delineate a nation   made only of hope.
It walks forward,
    always forward,

looking for houses   made of sugar and flour,
persimmons and apples. I watch

        myself go swimming
  in a river the opposite of loss,
    I watch my hands put coins in a beggar's cup,

I hear my mouth bequeath boats to refugees
    and promise exiles   that they will once again see their
  homeland.

I watch my hair   fly in the wind   like hundreds of freed sparrows
  rising,

    then we unite, body and whisper
of light
      the heart, o the heart
     forgetting how old it is
   offering itself to thorn bushes without any fear
believing there are many more houses,
      roofs intact, to live in.

ACKNOWLEDGMENTS

Grateful thanks to the editors of the following magazines in which some of the poems in this manuscript previously appeared:

8 Poems
"When the Night Comes In"
AlternaCtive PublicaCtions
"Why This"
"This Astonishing World"
"The House"
"The Houses"
"When the Night Comes In"
American Voice
"Lies"
Anatolios Magazine
"Lilies"
"Throw Yourself Like Water"
"Spirit, Give Me"
Collidescope
"All Forevers"
"Statues"
"In Rivers"
Inksounds
"Oracle"
Meniscus
"Ghazal"
Red Tree Review
"Enemies"
Smartish Pace
"The River"
SuperPresent
"Honey"
SurVision
"Lace"
"Marrow"
"Opposites"
The Windsor Review
"Crows"

"Descendant," "Lies," and "The Boat that Brought Sadness into the World" appeared in a chapbook, *The Gates of the Somnambulist*, published by Jeanne Duval Editions.

I wish to thank Rocio Aragon, Donald Bell, Timothy Dansdill, and Randy Watson who have been there since the very beginning for their invaluable friendship and encouragement. I wish to express my gratitude to Silvia Curbelo, Ed Hirsch, Kevin Prufer, and Victoria Tester (who has been there since my second beginning) for taking the time to read the book and provide meaningful comments. Richard Cantor and Andrea Lilienthal were there for me when I needed them most, and they remain important to me to this day. A special thanks to Sidney Mackenzie who knows why. With much appreciation, I want to acknowledge Donna Hughes for her inspiration in many forms. I send a giant hug to Elizabeth Josephson who is proof that friendship grows always through the years. My poetry teachers have always been important to me: in memory of Thomas Lux and Cynthia Macdonald who knew that the best teachers are those who see what a student is trying to do and help him or her do it. And, finally, a big hug and love to my husband for understanding that I need a room of my own to write in, for his undying support, and for taking care of matters large and small when I work in my poetry room.

Eva Skrande was born in Havana, Cuba and grew up in both Cuba and Miami, Florida. She has a BA from Sarah Lawrence College, an MFA from the Iowa Writers' Workshop, and a PhD from the Graduate Program in Creative Writing and Literature at the University of Houston. Skrande is the author of two volumes of poems, including *My Mother's Cuba* (River City Poetry Series) and *Bone Argot* (Spuyten Duyvil Press) as well as a chapbook, *The Gates of the Somnambulist* (Jeanne Duval Editions). Her poems have appeared in *Agni, The Iowa Review, Smartish Pace, The American Poetry Review,* and elsewhere. Skrande has received fellowships from the Creative Writing Program at the University of Houston, the Inprint Foundation, and the Houston Arts Council. She teaches Poetry Writing and Creative Writing to people of all ages. She is also a faculty tutor at Houston Community College and a writing coach at Write for Success Tutoring. She lives in Houston with her husband and daughter.

www.ingramcontent.com/pod-product-compliance
Lightning Source LLC
Chambersburg PA
CBHW020341170426
43200CB00006B/457